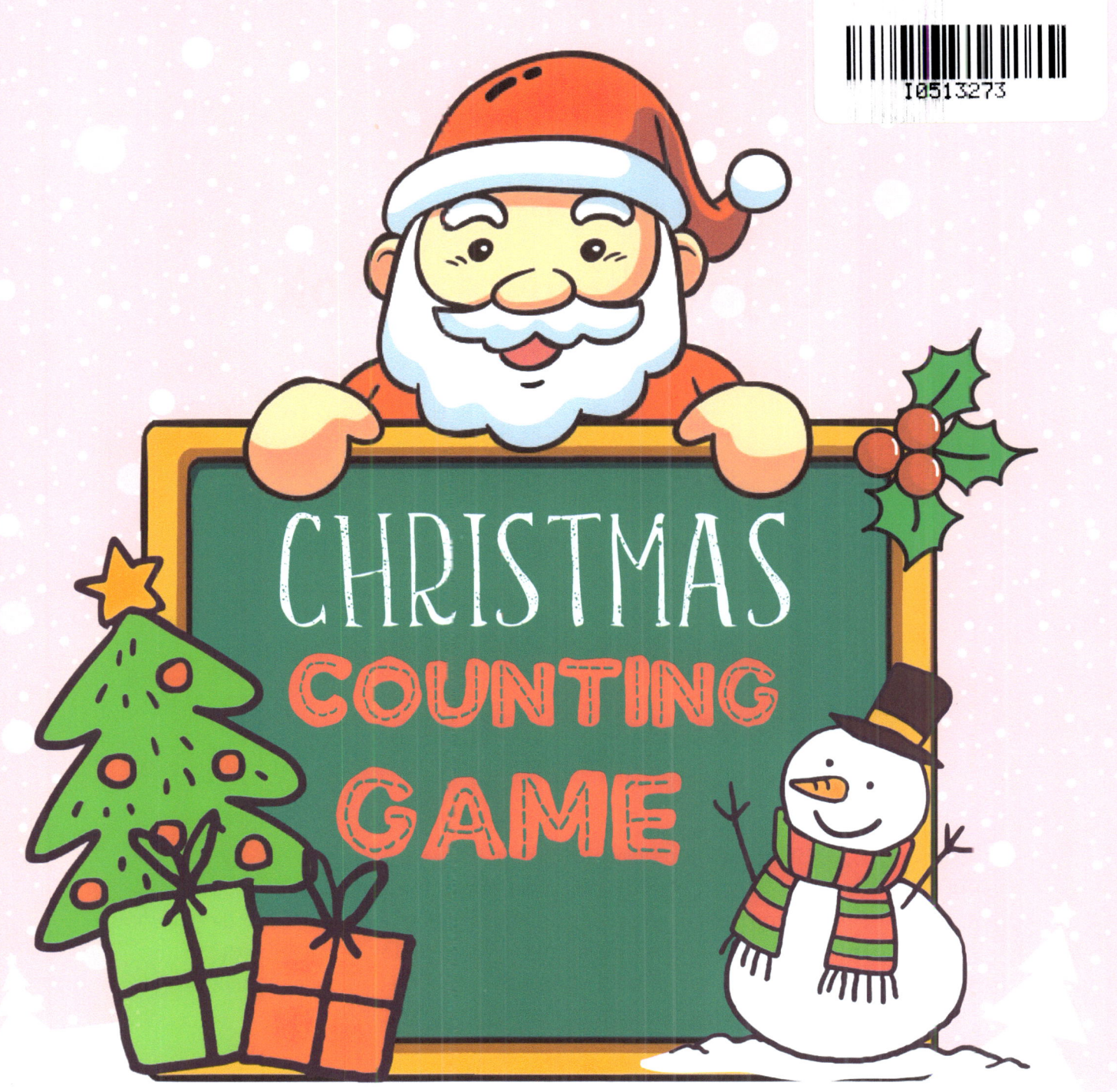

Enjoy this Notebook?

Please leave us a review as we would love to hear your reviews, thoughts, and advice in order to create better products and services for you.

Thank you for your support.

Copyright © 2019 by Little Kids Creative Press
All rights reserved. No part of this publication may be reproduced, distributed, or transmitted in any form or by any means, including photocopying, recording, or other electronic or mechanical methods, without the prior written permission of the publisher, except in the case of brief quotations embodied in critical reviews and certain other noncommercial uses permitted by copyright law.

Let's count THE SNOWMANS

THERE ARE

2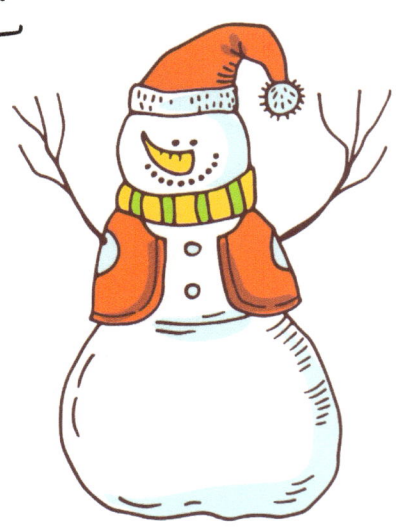

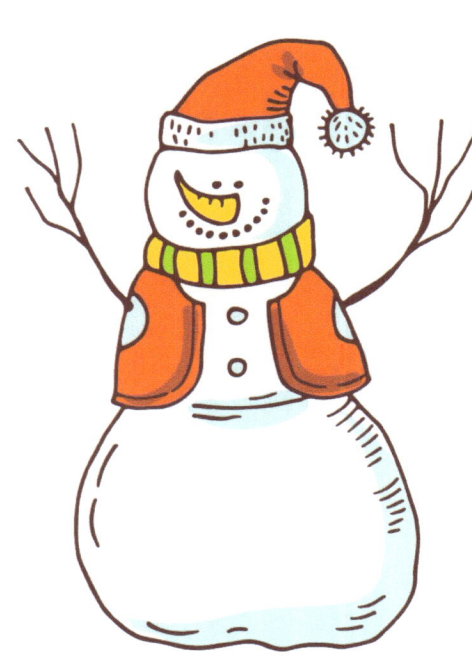 SNOWMAN

Let's count
THE GINGERBREADS

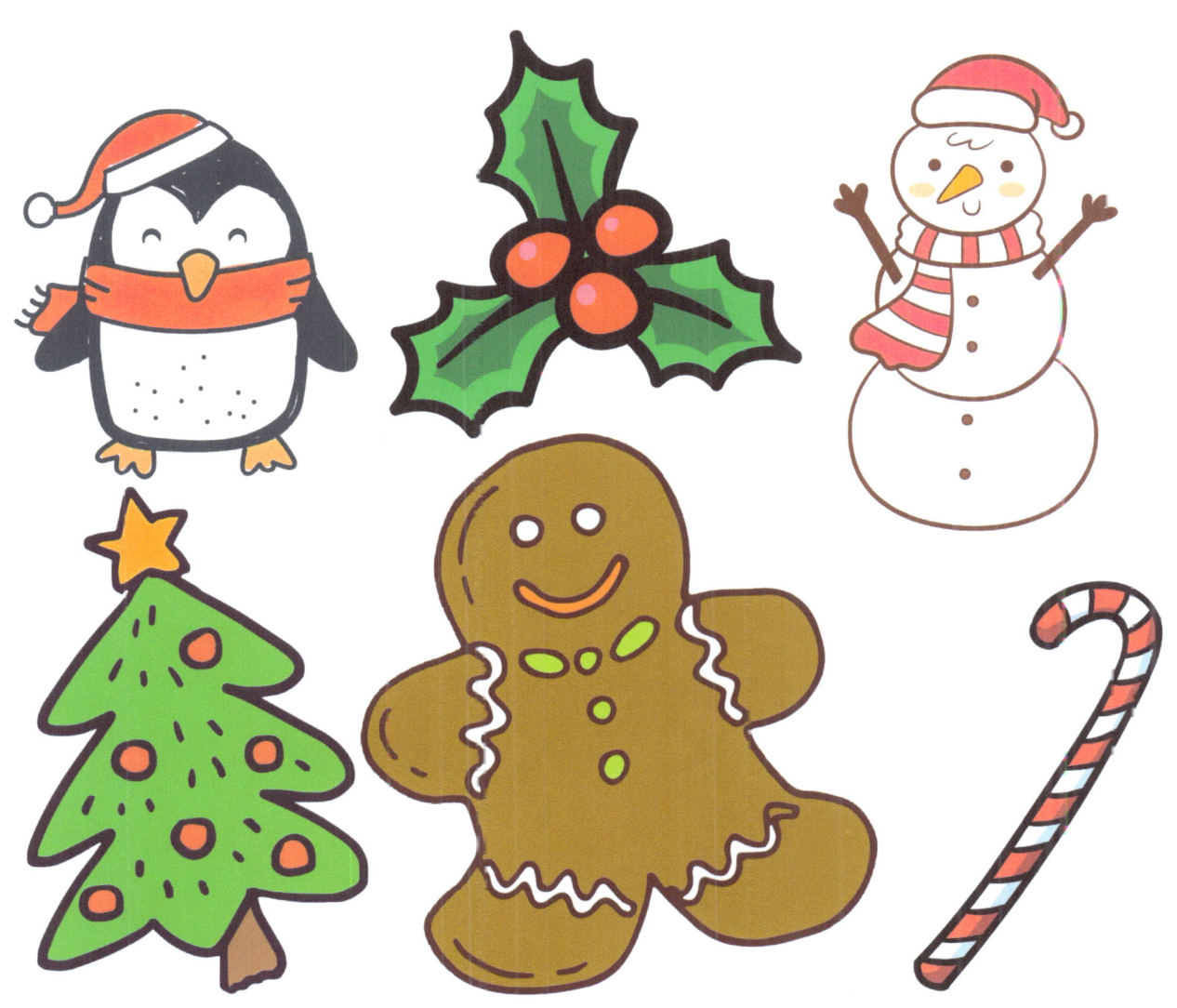

THERE IS

1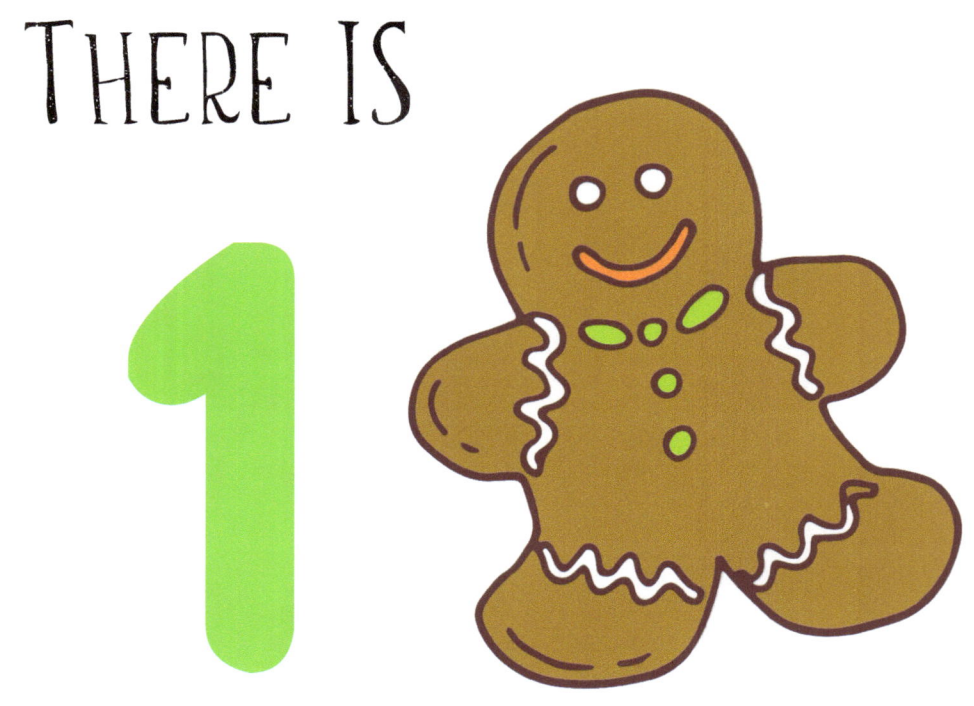

GINGERBREAD

Let's count THE ELVES

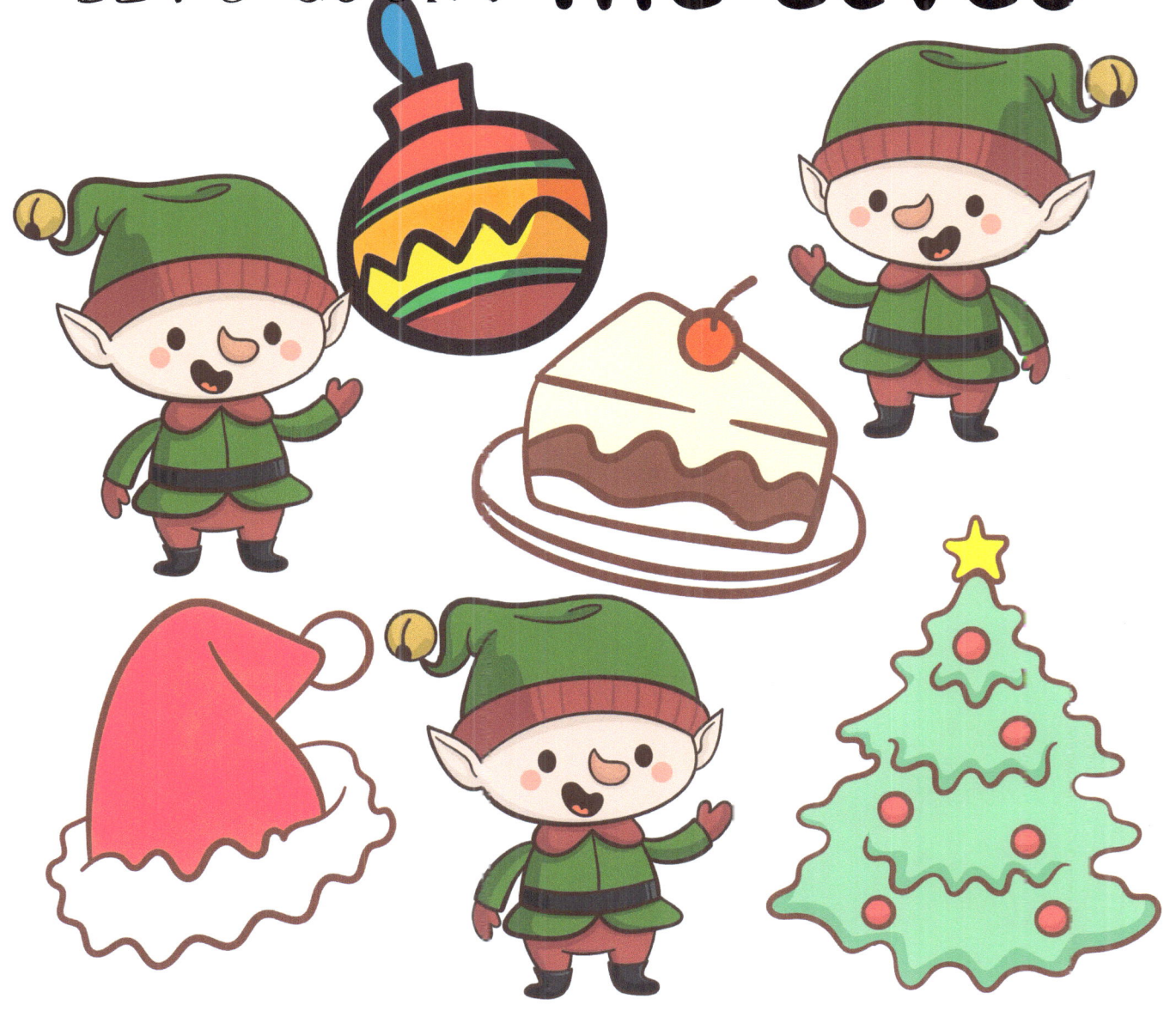

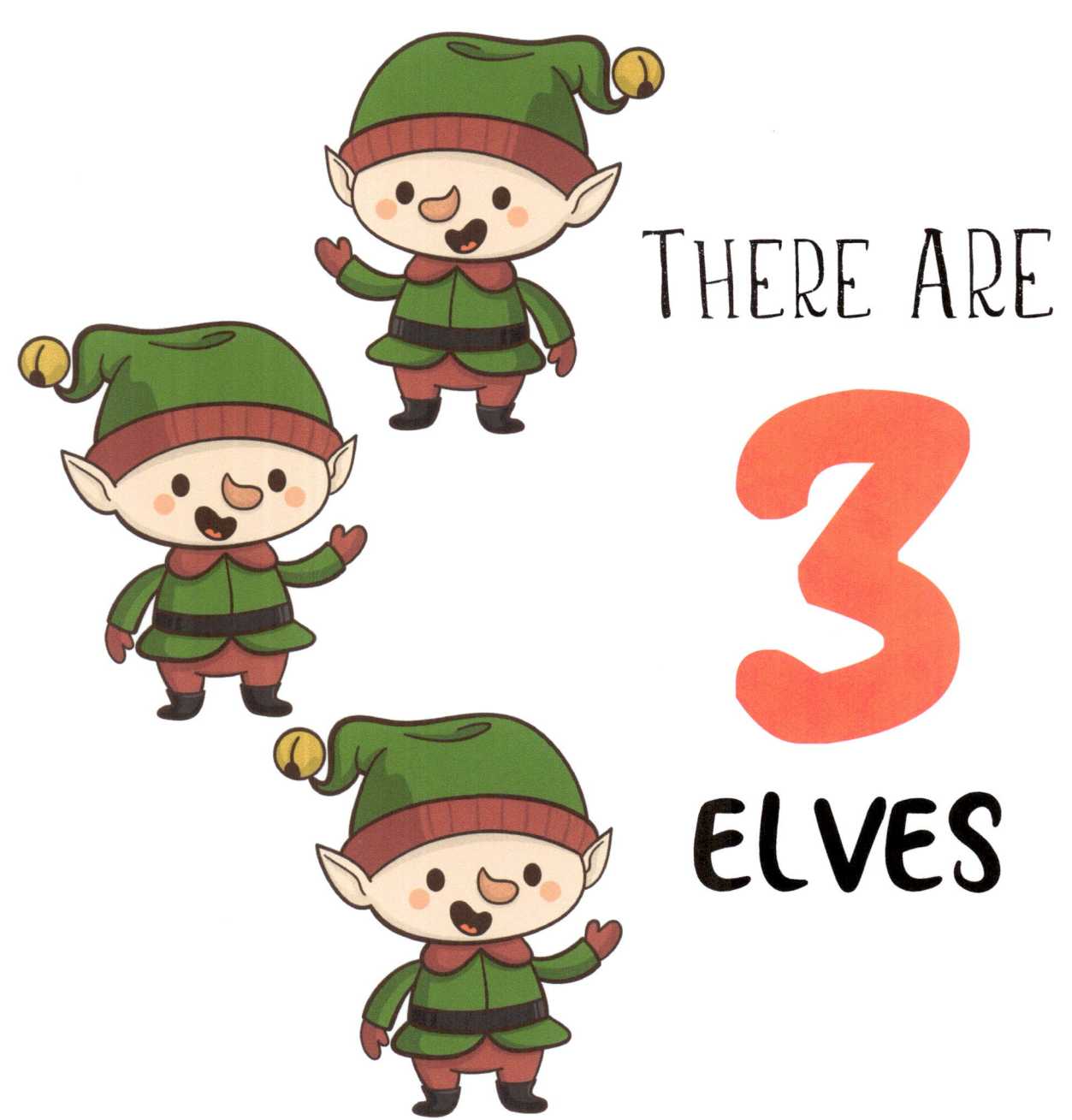

Let's count
The Christmas Trees

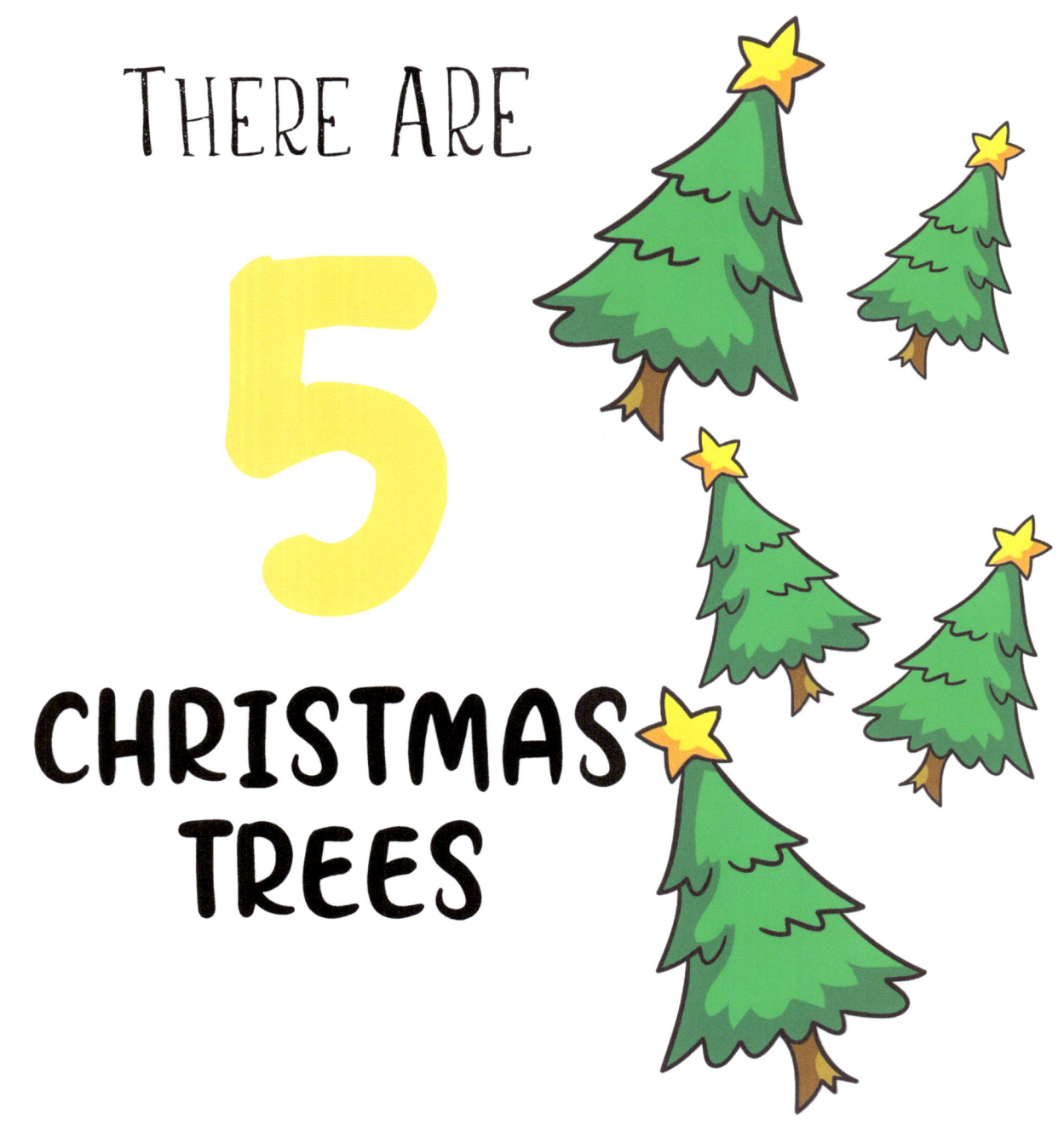

THERE ARE 5 CHRISTMAS TREES

Let's count THE STOCKINGS

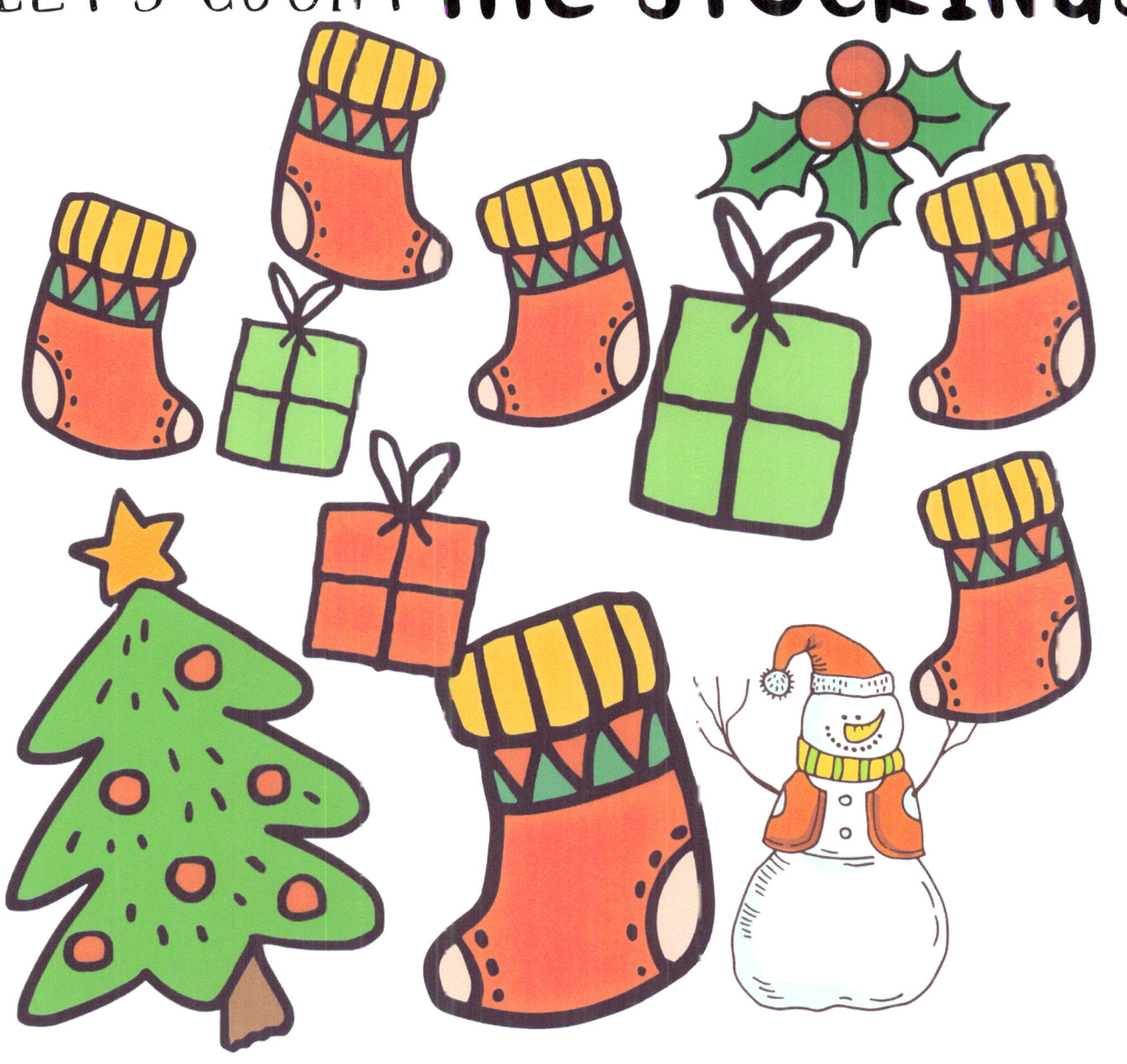

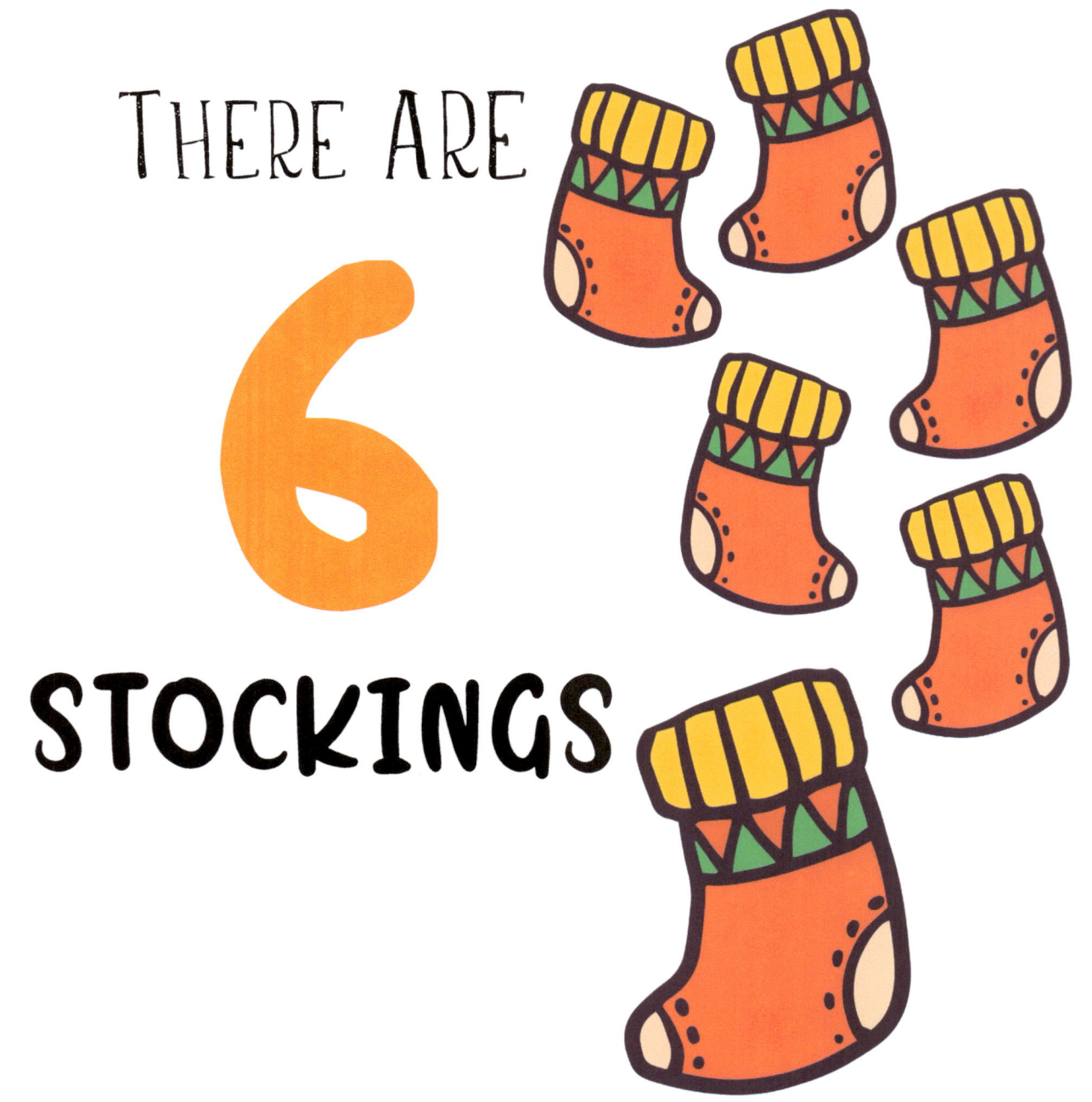

THERE ARE 6 STOCKINGS

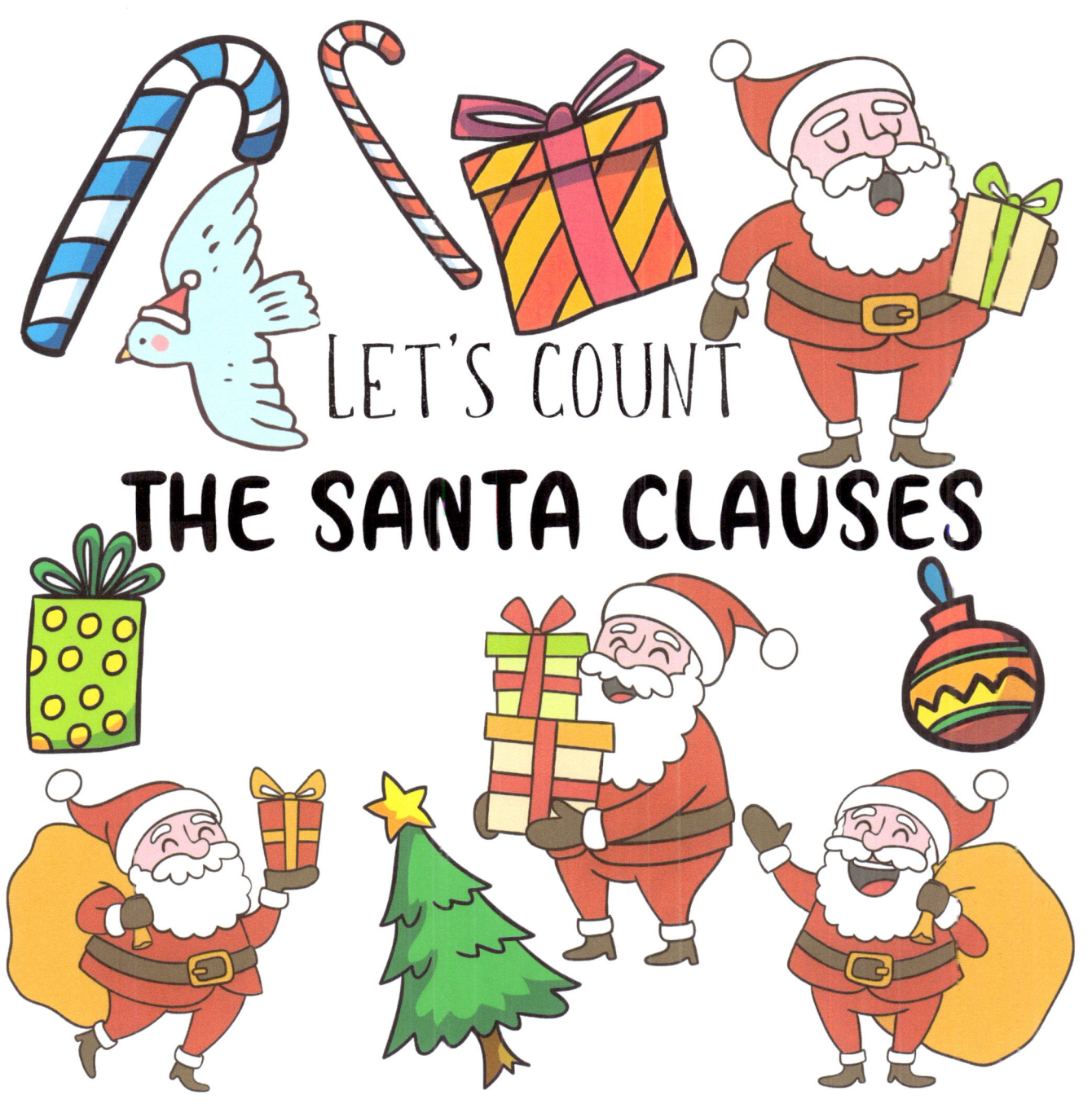

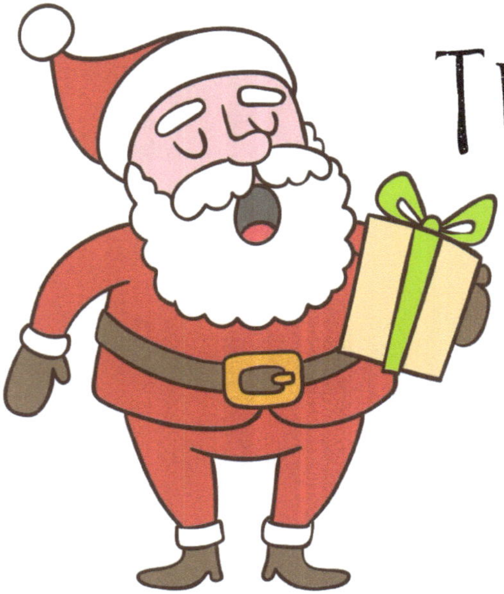

THERE ARE 4 SANTA CLAUS

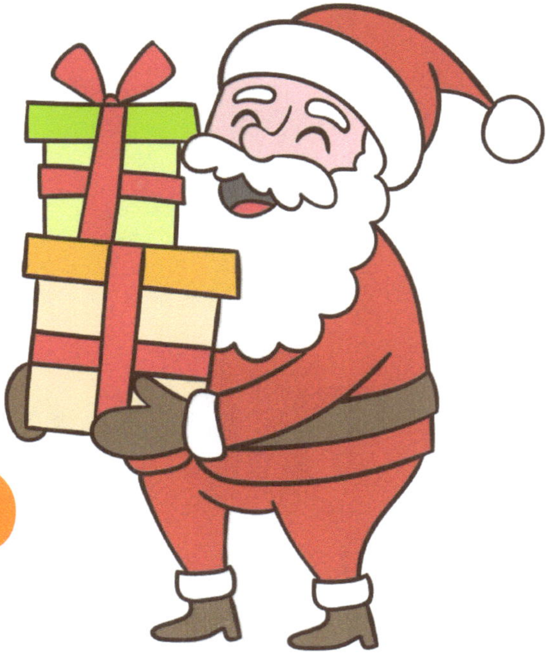

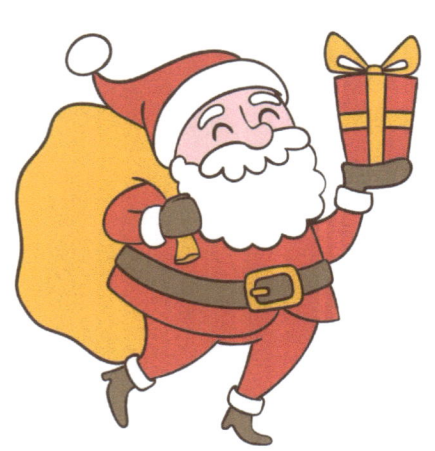
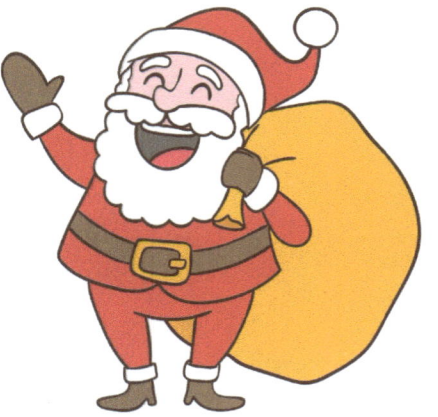

Let's count the snowglobes

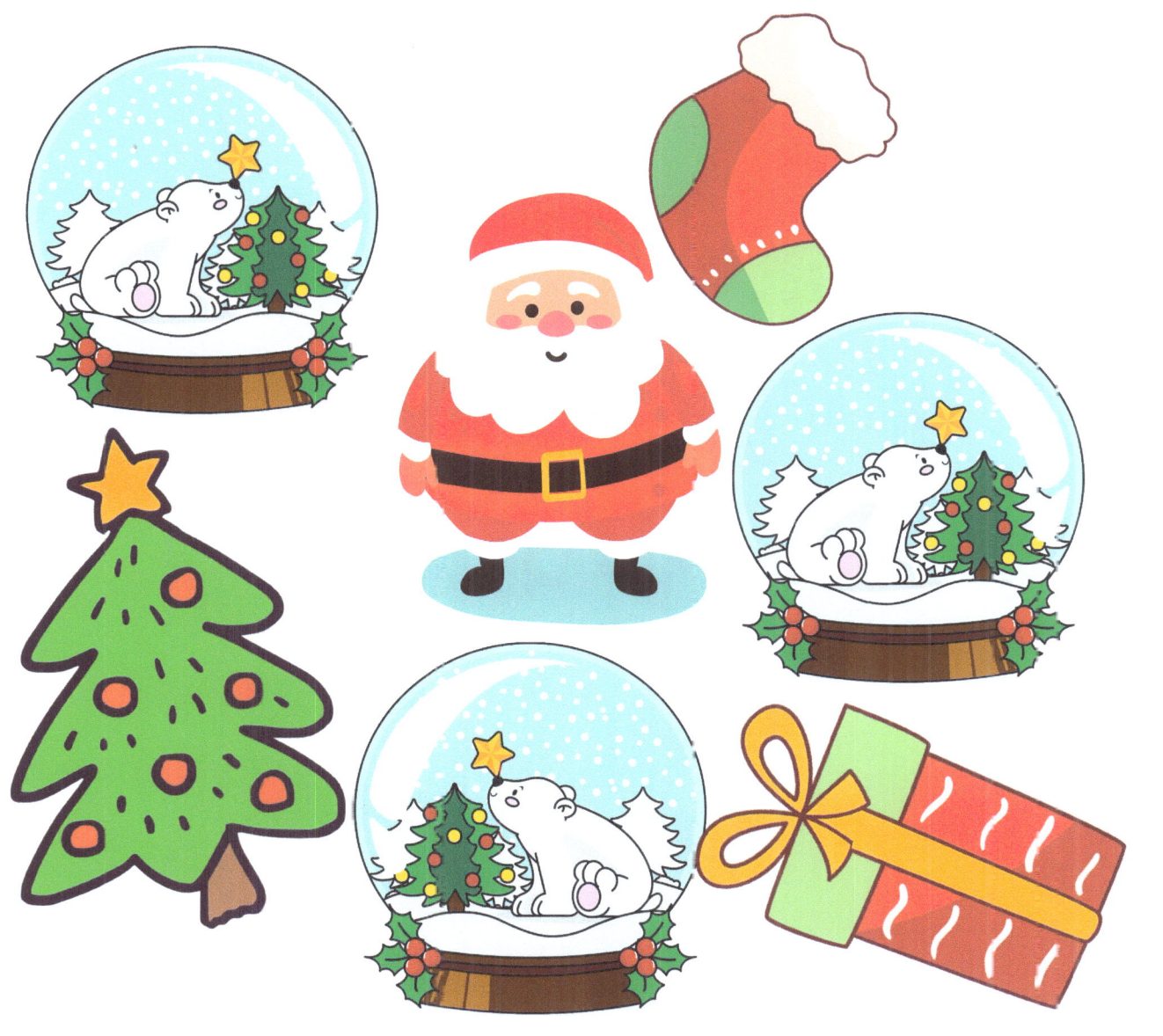

THERE ARE

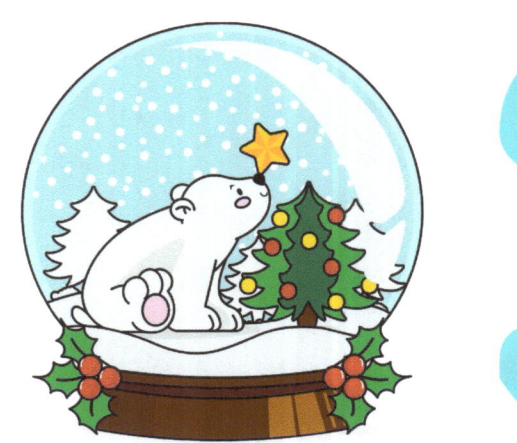 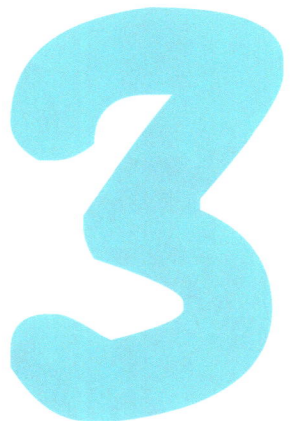 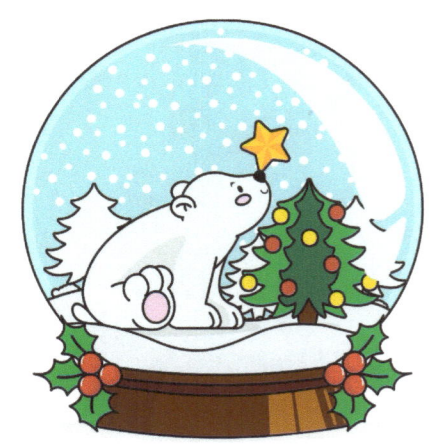

SNOWGLOBES

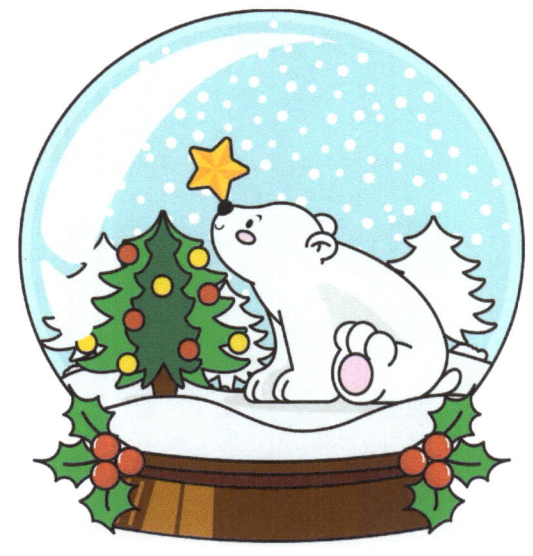

Let's count the penguins

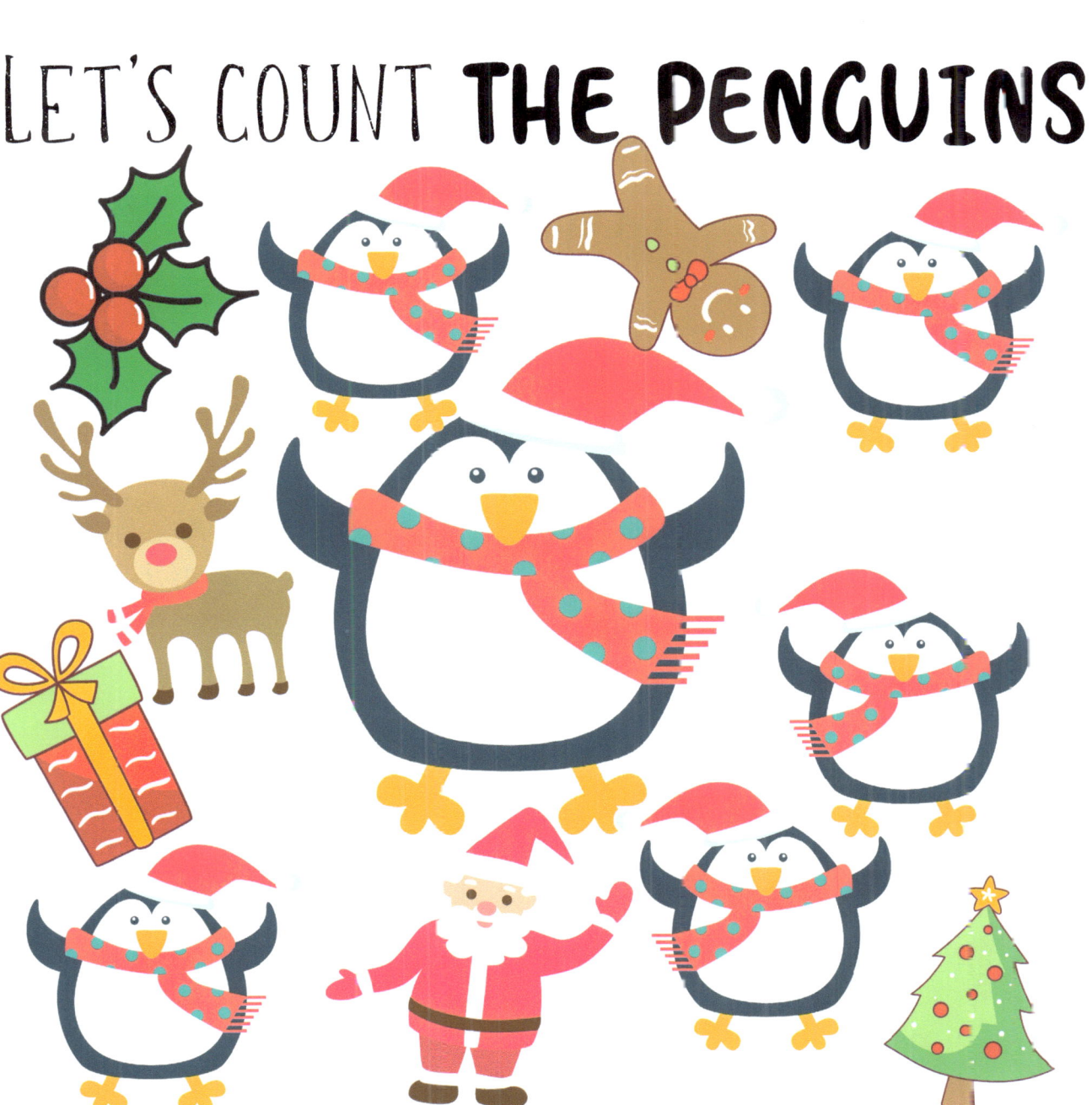

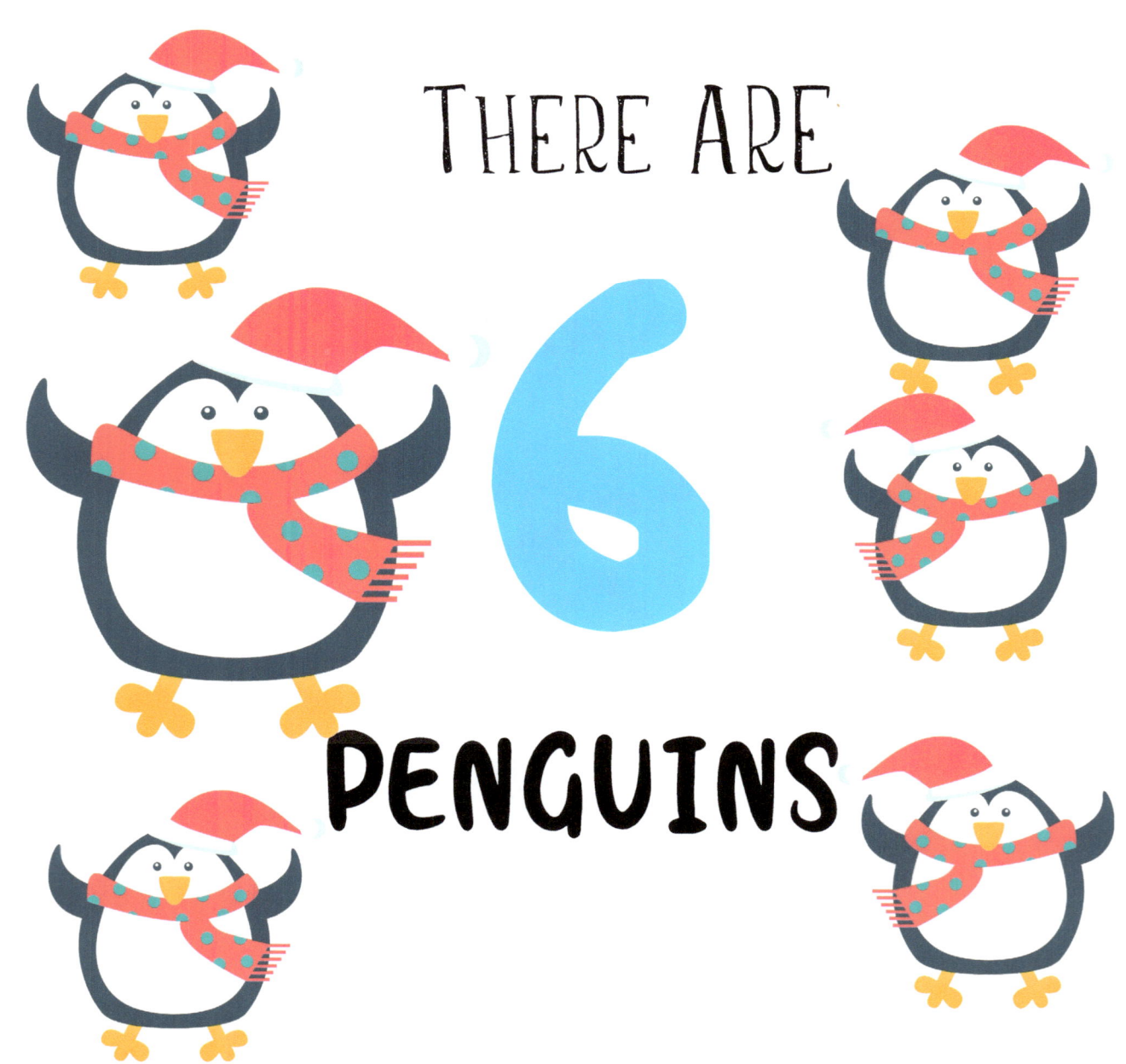

Let's count the reindeers

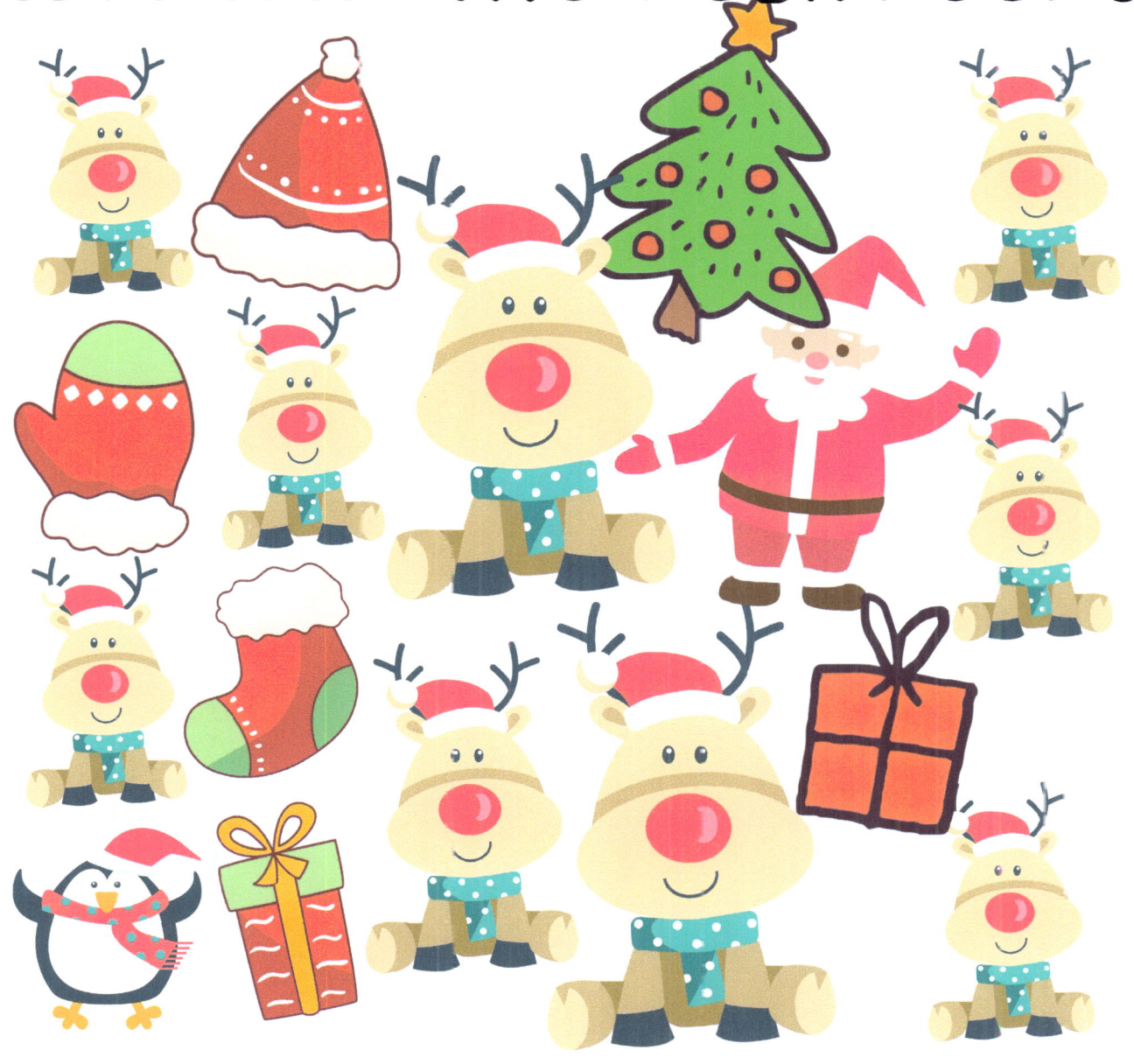

THERE ARE **9** REINDEERS

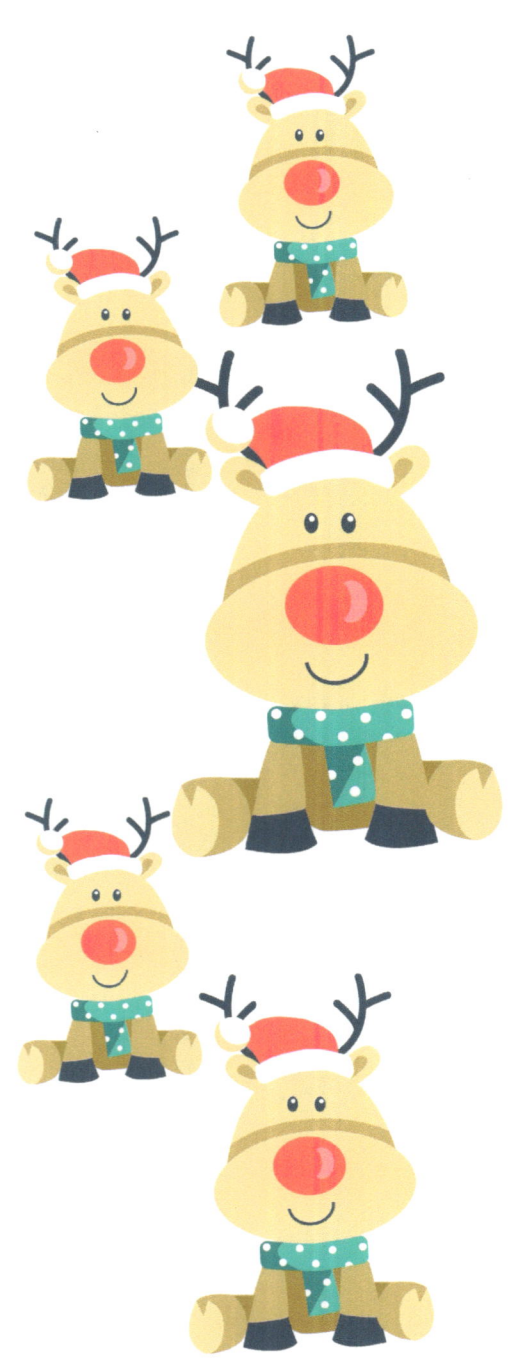
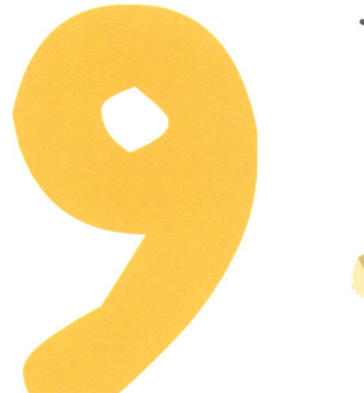

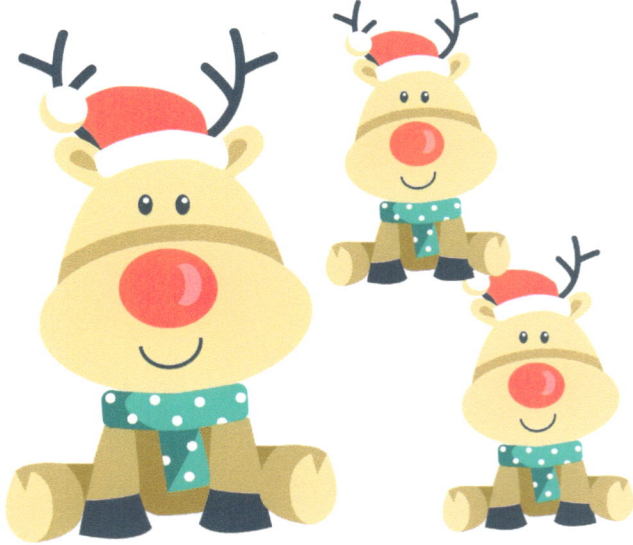

Let's count the presents

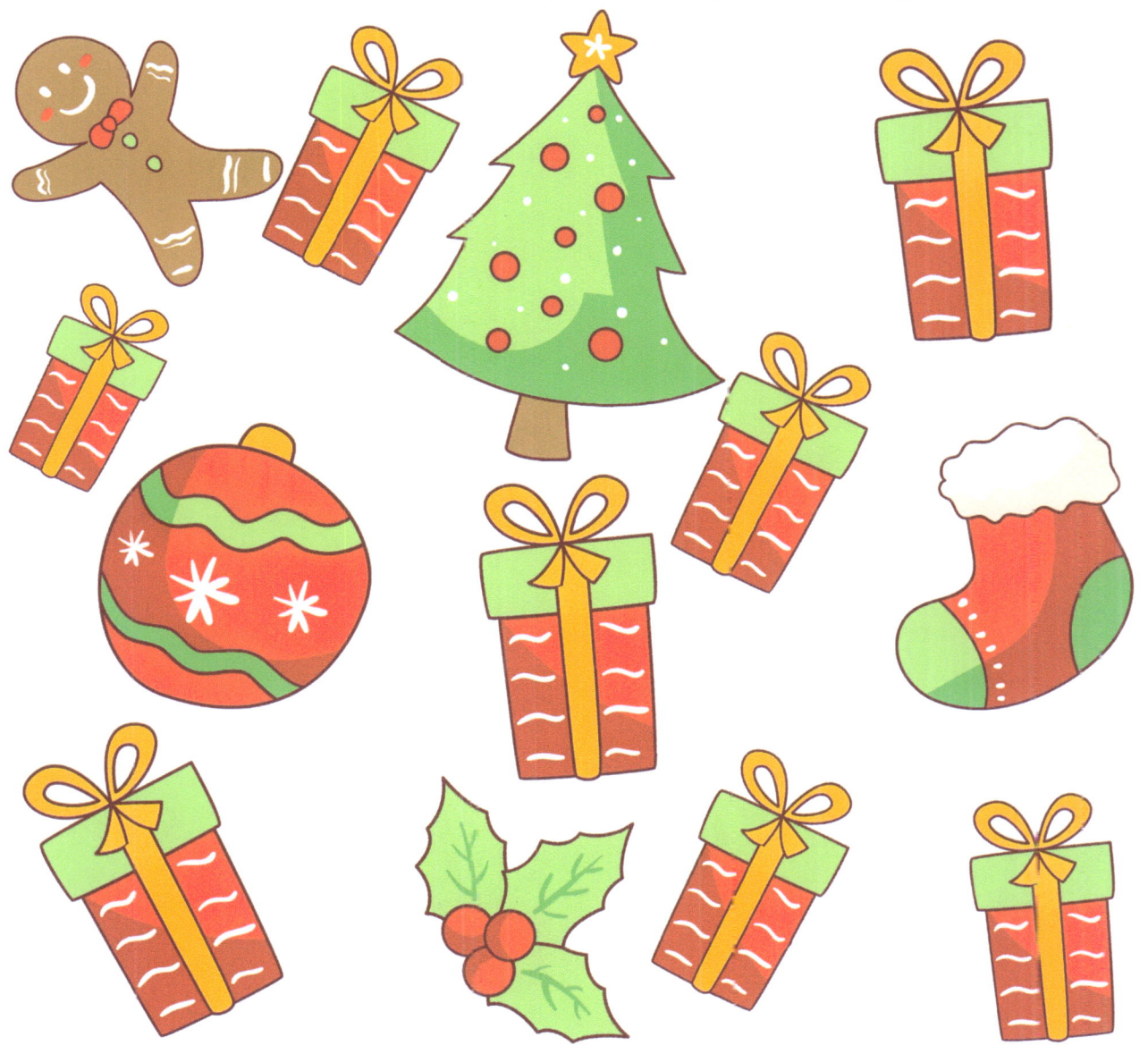

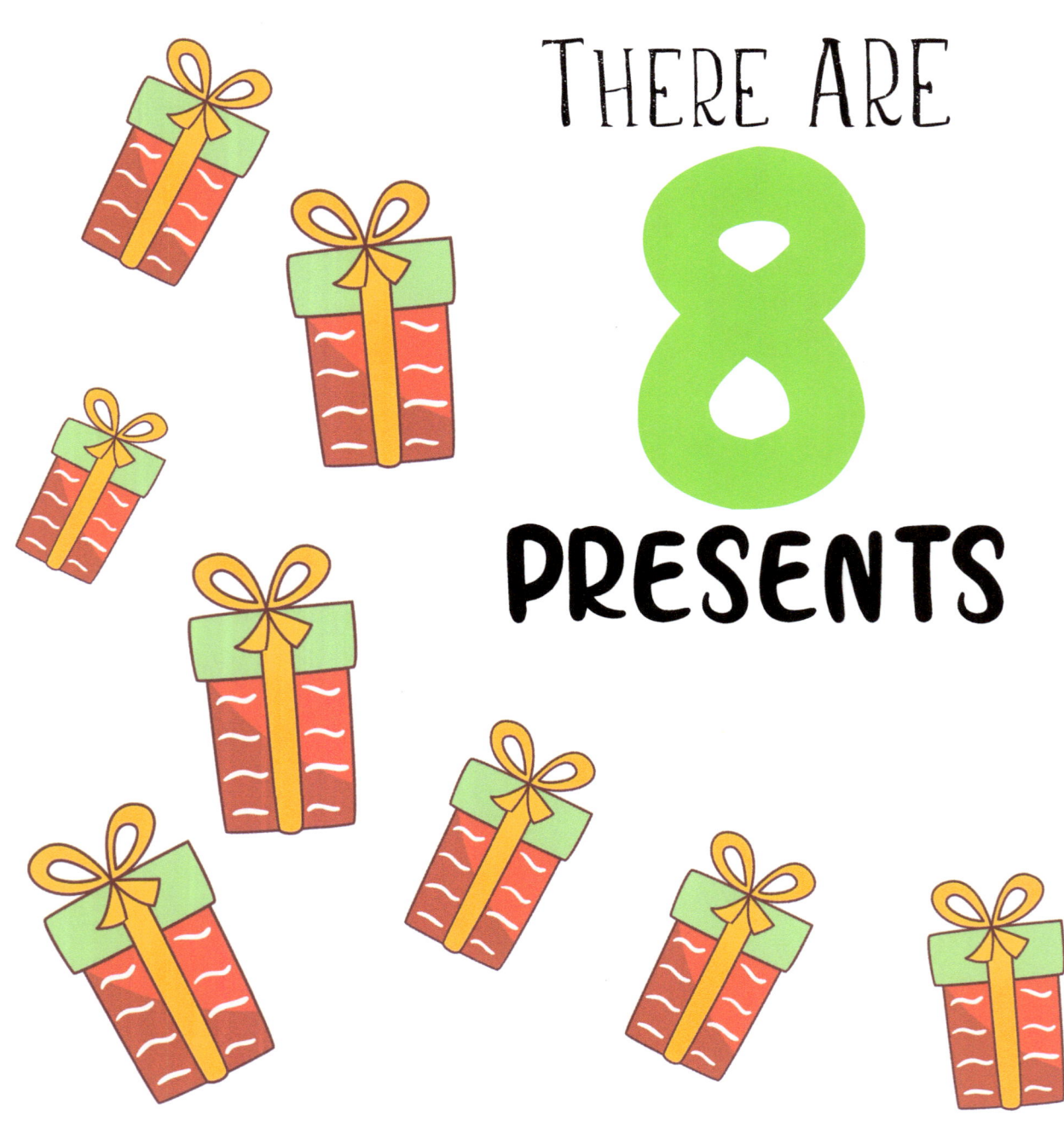

Let's count THE ANGELS

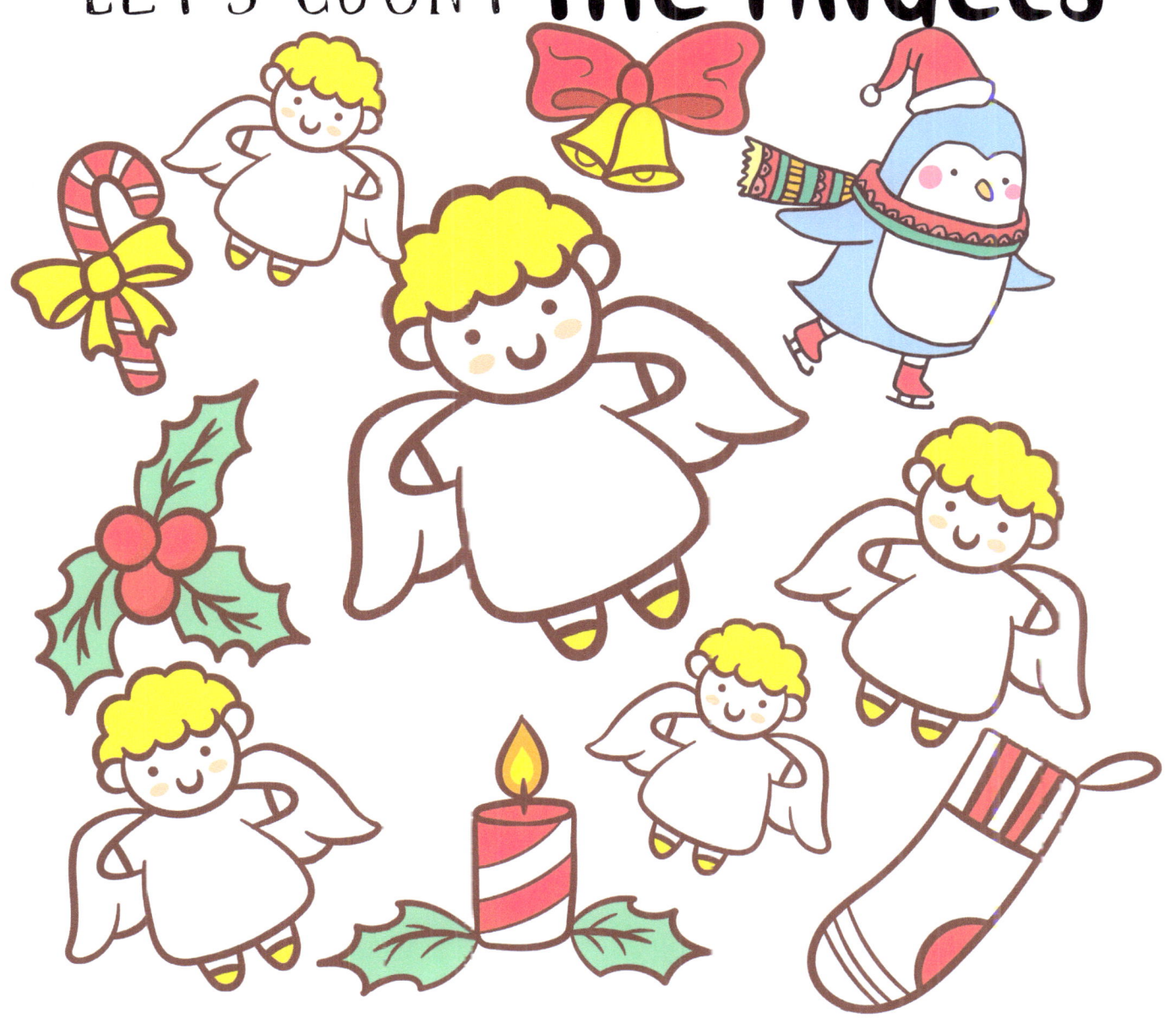

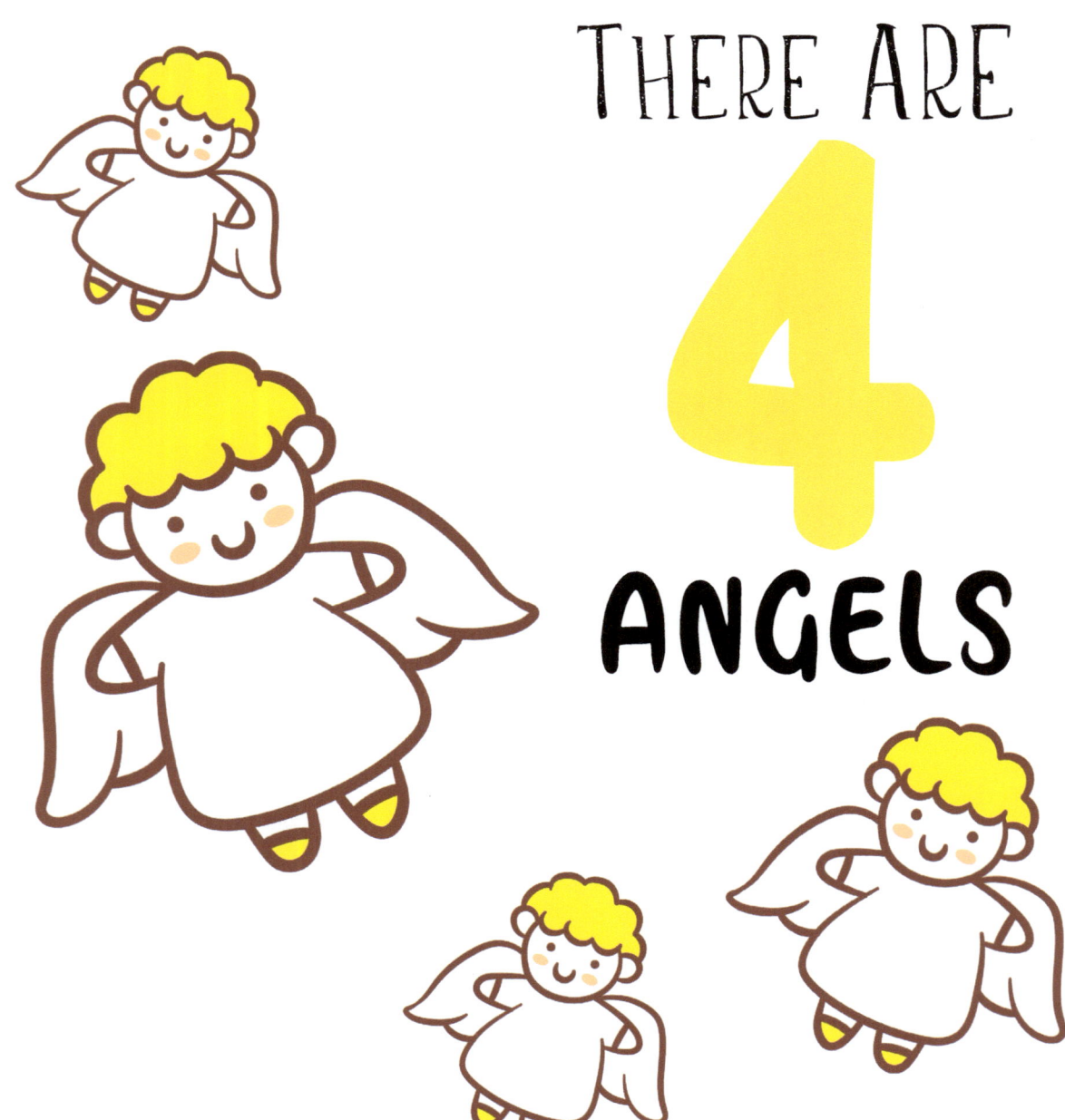

HOW MANY PRESENTS ON THE SANTA HANDS?

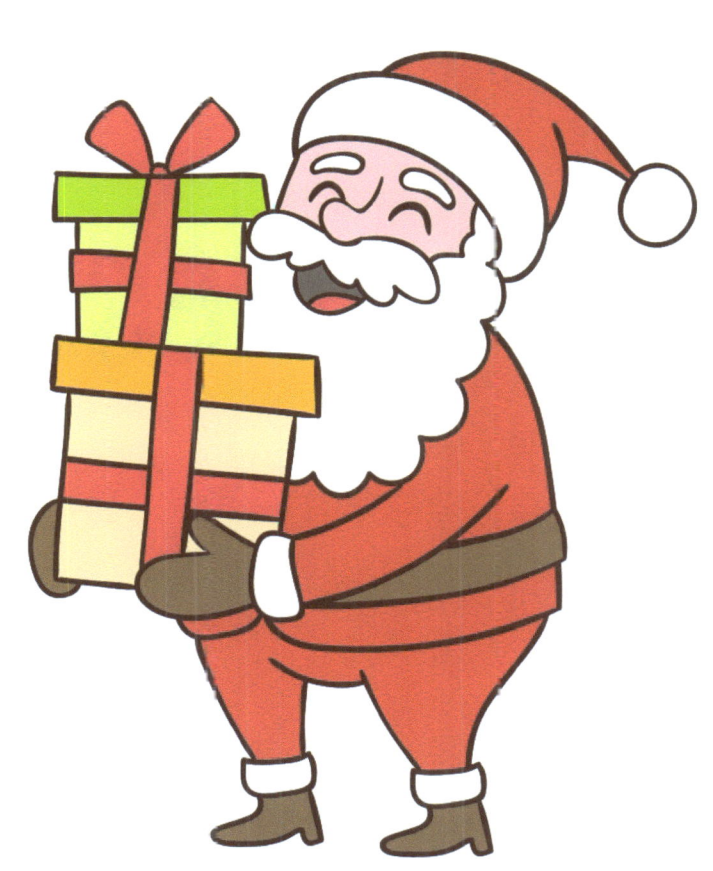

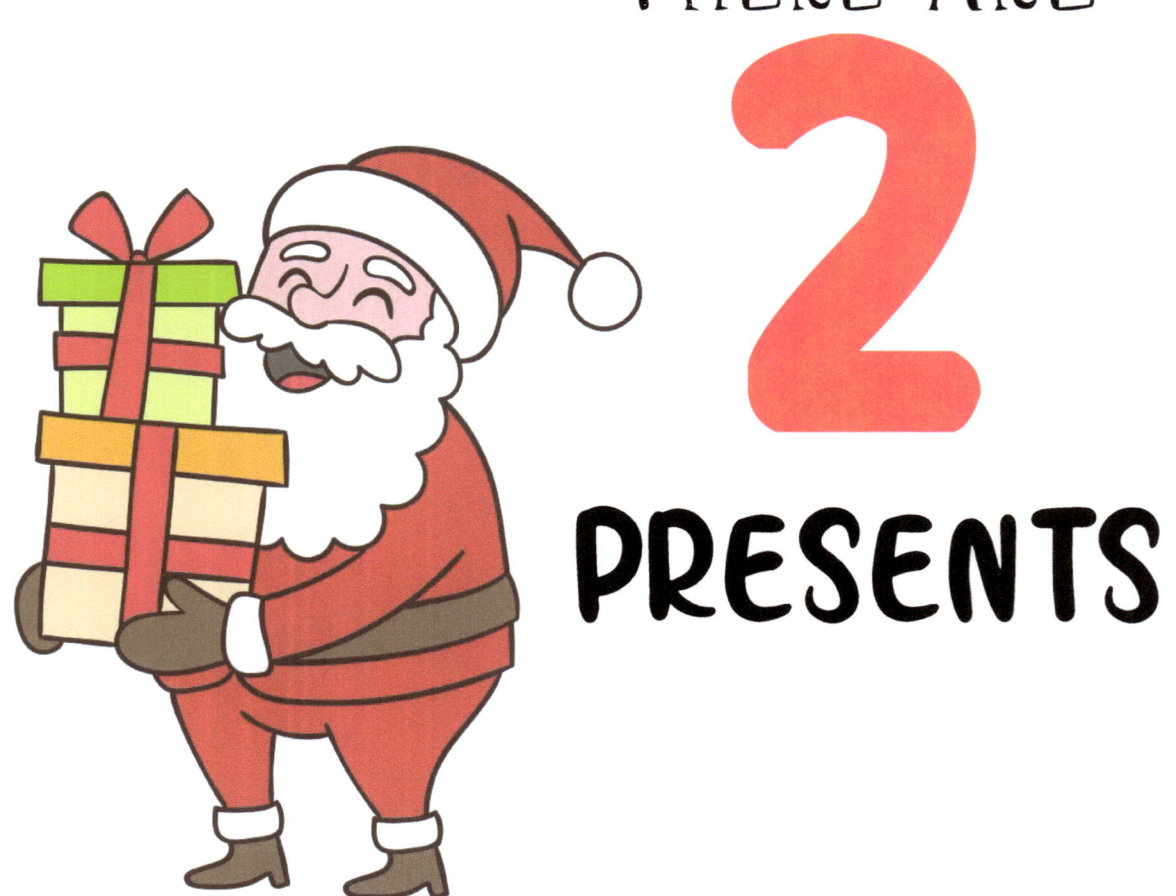

HOW MANY PRESENTS ON THE SANTA HANDS?

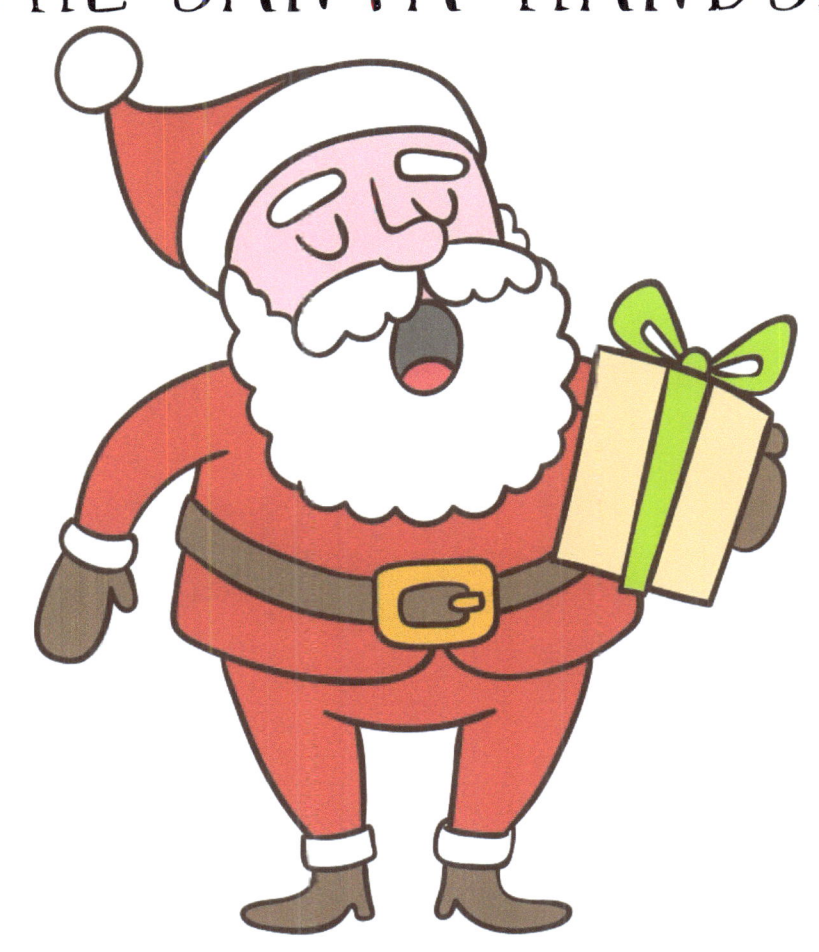

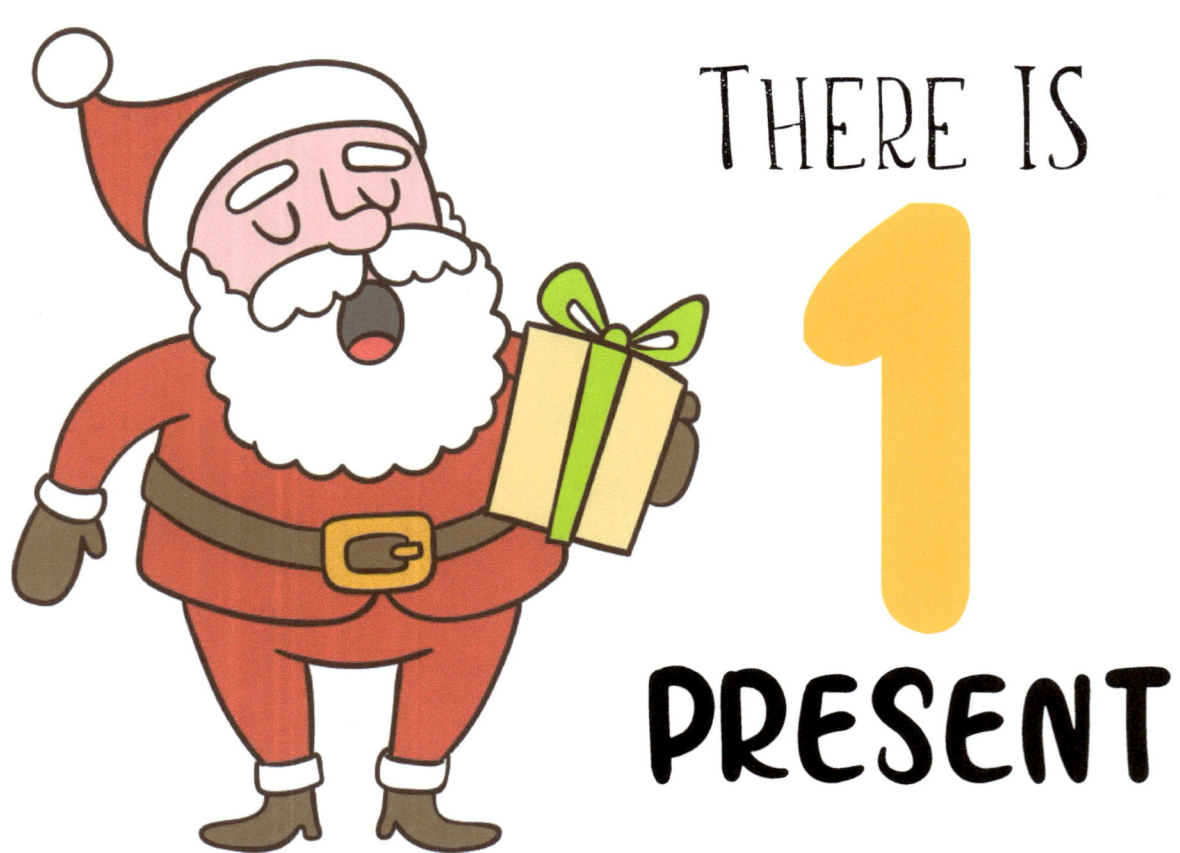

HOW MANY POLAR BEAR IN THE SNOWGLOBE?

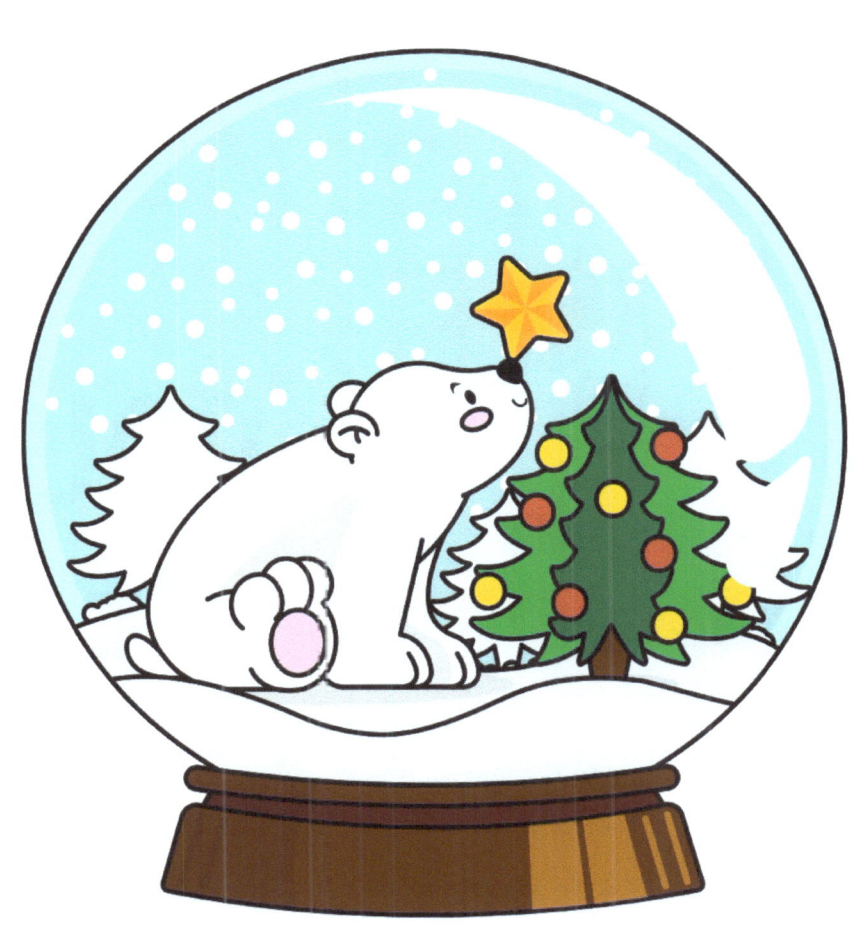

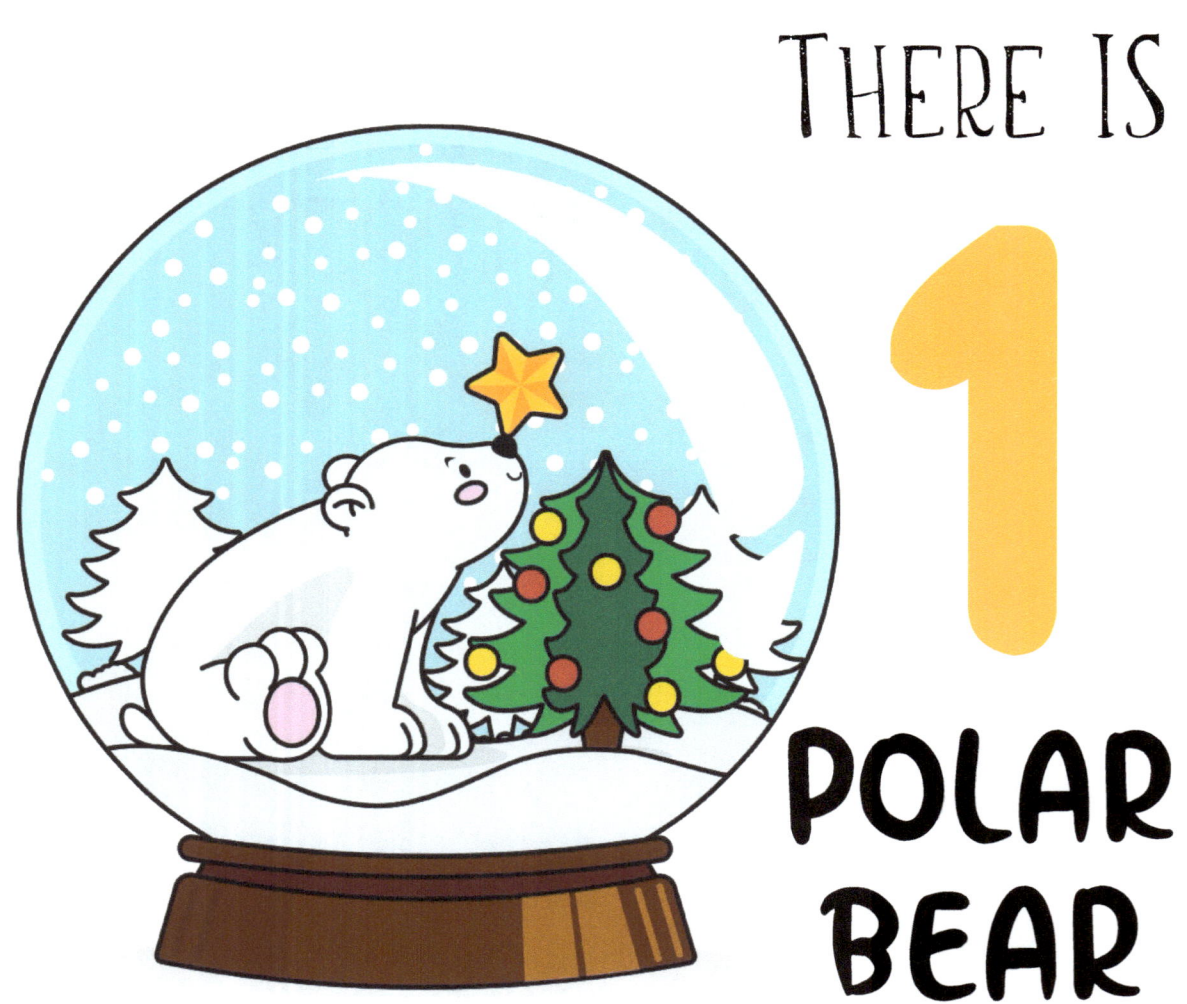

THERE IS **1** POLAR BEAR

HOW MANY CHIRSTMAS TREE ON THE BEAR HANDS?

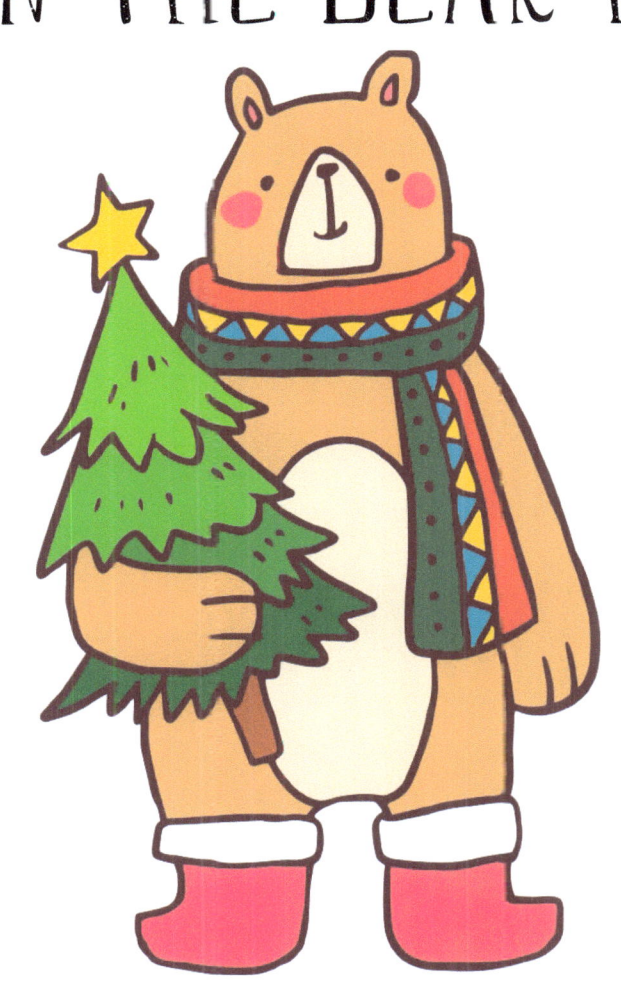

THERE IS **1** CHIRSTMAS TREE

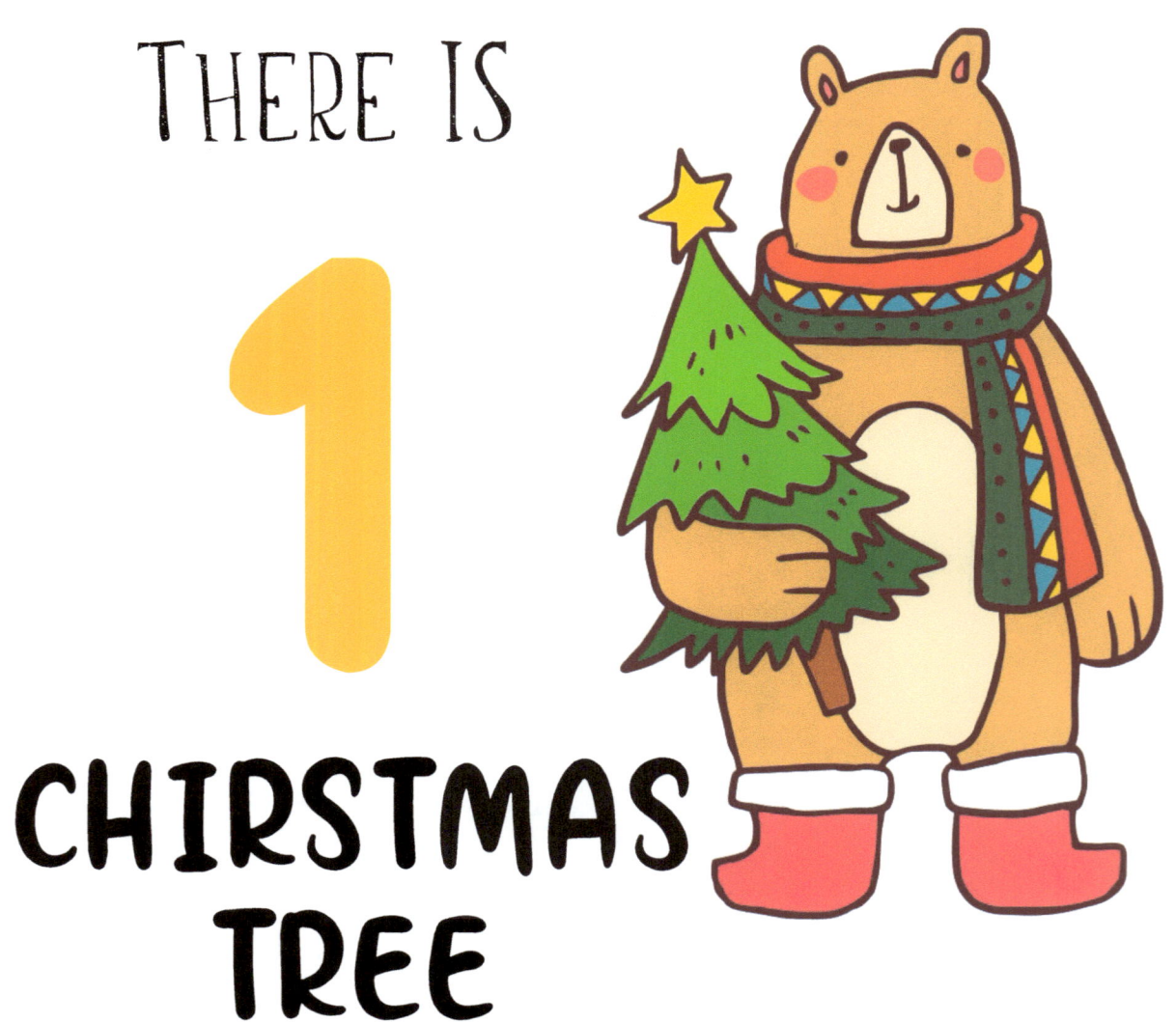

www.ingramcontent.com/pod-product-compliance
Lightning Source LLC
Chambersburg PA
CBHW051821210526
45473CB00005B/1693